Called to Duty

How We Stayed Together While We Were Apart

Nancy Jo Sutton-McLeod

Bloomington, IN  Milton Keynes, UK

AuthorHouse™
1663 Liberty Drive, Suite 200
Bloomington, IN 47403
www.authorhouse.com
Phone: 1-800-839-8640

AuthorHouse™ *UK Ltd.*
500 Avebury Boulevard
Central Milton Keynes, MK9 2BE
www.authorhouse.co.uk
Phone: 08001974150

© 2006 Nancy Jo Sutton-McLeod. All rights reserved.

No part of this book may be reproduced, stored in a retrieval system, or transmitted by any means without the written permission of the author.

First published by AuthorHouse 5/4/2006

ISBN: 1-4259-2655-X (sc)

Printed in the United States of America
Bloomington, Indiana

This book is printed on acid-free paper.

Title: ON DEATH AND DYING
Author: Elisabeth Kubler-Ross
ISBN: 0-02-605060-9 / 0-684-83938-5
Selection: Scattered quotations from PP. 53, 99-100, 124-125, and "The Five Stages of Grief – Grief, Anger, Bargaining, Depression, Acceptance"

To mom, dad, and my soldier

Table of Contents

Introduction	ix
Getting the Call	1
Saying Goodbye	19
Living Alone	31
Leave	49
He's Coming Home	63
Settling in Again	99
References	109

Introduction

I am this new independent, if a little imperfect, woman. I have managed to handle everything, from installing blinds to getting a building permit for a new patio. Having never lived by myself, I was surprised to make it as long as a year. I know I am not alone and that there are thousands of women across the country that have been through the same thing; however, I still can't help feeling like I am the only one that has been put through this kind of test and survived. Luckily he's back ... but what now?

I thought homecoming would be the greatest time of my life -- so why are we fighting all the time? For some reason we don't feel comfortable talking to each other about our feelings any more. It seems like we are walking on eggshells because we don't want to ruin the honeymoon we are "supposed" to be experiencing. Why aren't I happy to have my husband back from Iraq?

This is not just my experience. People who have dealt with deployment before told me quite frequently, that the homecoming was harder than the sending off. I didn't believe them. I could not imagine that it would be worse to finally have my husband home. I had the romantic notion that love conquers all and nothing could be worse than being separated from my soul mate. I was wrong.

Now we are managing and changing and adapting. These are things we have learned well over the last year. The deployment and redeployment process is a rollercoaster and we will both be forever changed by this experience. It is something that most military families have to deal with when a loved one is deployed. The joy and pain, twists and turns, and ups and downs can make a couple stronger if they are willing to learn from them. My husband and I have found that my silly romantic notion of

Called to Duty

all-powerful love might not be so silly after all. Love just needs a little help getting over the hump in the attempt to conquer all.

By gaining perspective of what the deployment and reunion has taught us, it is possible to develop a stronger connection in our marriage. This connection is essential for a National Guard couple since deployment is always a possibility. Going away once does not guarantee your soldier will not go away again. Therefore, as a soldier's wife, it is your duty to survive the separation and reunion, and to work with your husband to strengthen your bond. After all, he is fighting for you and your family.

I tried to keep it together while he was gone, and now that he is back, I am constantly working on reconnecting with him. I learned the hard way what works and what does not. I had very few people to draw expertise from given that I did not know anyone who had shared my experience. I think the most helpful resource would have been someone who had endured a similar deployment and reunion.

This book is intended to tell my story. I want to let others know they are not alone. I want to help couples appreciate the important lessons that I gained from each step of the deployment process, with the hope that they do the same. Even if you have not dealt with a deployment or are not in the military, the lessons are valuable for a meaningful connection in your marriage, especially when there are times when you must be apart. These lessons have applications over a wide range of relationships. A lot of the issues I had to deal with are common to both military and non-military spouses alike. It is my intention that you find some similarities in your life and apply my hard-learned lessons to your relationships. I felt lost and hopeless when I was thrown into this situation. I only hope that I can provide guidance to women who feel the same as I did.

In order to understand the full importance of each lesson, I should begin with the storm brewing before the deployment. By progressing through the stages, you can learn tricks and information to help through each phase involved in a military deployment. I believe that the homecoming is the hardest part, so laying a good foundation in the beginning can save a lot of heartache in the end. Here is my story.

Getting the Call

Before and during the deployment, the relationship goes through a number of mutations. After these changes, most couples do not realize that their relationship cannot be the same. A couple cannot continue with the same patterns of interactions and intimacy when their worldview is about to dramatically transform. It all starts when the soldier is called to duty.

In my case, I had only two days notice. He was called first for a communications unit, but told that he was not qualified and could not go. Shortly thereafter, he was called again, this time for a transportation unit. In these four hours, I experienced an incredible rollercoaster of emotion. First he was going then he was not. This uncertainty left me feeling completely powerless and victimized. I was being forced to experience something I did not want to and I had no power to stop it.

The only thing I remember after hearing the news was complete numbness. I knew I should be feeling some really strong emotions, but I couldn't feel anything. The emotional shock had set in. My husband wanted a response from me and I didn't know what to say. I couldn't think clearly even though I knew there were a lot of decisions that needed to be made immediately. I kept thinking that I was in a dream and that this wasn't really happening.

When I finally woke up a few moments later, an intense fear took over. There were so many things to be scared of and I was feeling them all simultaneously. How long will he be gone? Is it dangerous where he is going? Will our relationship last through a yearlong separation? Will he cheat on me? Will I be tempted to cheat on him? What if he gets hurt? What if he dies? What in the world is going on and what is going to happen to us? I couldn't concentrate with all of these issues floating around in my head. I picked up my rosary, which I had not used since I was a little girl, and starting saying prayers. It was the only thing I could do to prevent myself from losing my mind.

Once my head was put back together, I moved into denial. Initially, I reasoned that like the Gulf War, this conflict would be over before it started. It might not last long enough for him to even get over there. I rationed that he would be home before the end of his one-year term. I found enough reasons to convince myself that the situation would not be dangerous and he would not be gone long. The war had not even started yet so I had no reason to believe that this was going to be a big deal. My denial produced a calming effect, which enabled me to help my husband make the preparations necessary to deploy.

Many people give denial a bad rap, but I found it can be helpful in small doses. By definition, denial is a coping mechanism; it allows you to accomplish what you need to do in order to get by. Denial can be harmful when people cling to it unnecessarily. Many beneficial things, done excessively, can end up being harmful. Even water, if consumed in excess, can be poisonous to your body. In my case, there were a million things to get done in a short amount of time and my shock and fear were not allowing anything to be accomplished. When in denial, I could cope with the situation and set my other feelings aside. After I packed my husband's bags, signed the paperwork, and finished the other routine tasks, it was time to brace myself for the deployment.

Maybe my situation is a little different from other wives. I was against my husband joining the military at all. I knew that I could not handle him being gone and could not fathom carrying on while he was called off to war. Being the reasonable woman I am I did not give him an ultimatum. I did not want to force him to do something he did not want to do. I did not want to confront his resentment later on, had I forced him to choose. He decided to join, but chose a unit that rarely gets activated. Obviously that has no bearing with how things exploded in Iraq, but who could foresee that?

In my sudden shock and grief, I could feel resentment starting to build up inside me. After all, his decision to join the armed forces was against my wishes. It took a while for me to realize that I had a choice too, and I chose to marry a part-time soldier. When he received his orders, I could not recognize the mass of resentment mounting inside me. I believed that it was just my frustration with the situation. I did not realize my anger was directed towards him until I found myself blaming him for leaving.

At this period it became very clear that I had not been honest with myself. I thought that I could change my husband or some how control what would happen to our future; but these were impossible goals. Learning to be honest with myself and relinquishing control were the first two lessons I had to learn.

Lesson One

Being honest with yourself is the only way to truly connect with another person. People often enter into relationships with preconceived notions and expectations. This is a normal and human thing to do. We all have hopes and dreams about the future. It is when we let those ideas cloud our vision that we lie to ourselves.

The dishonesty starts with denial. I was in complete denial that the National Guard would affect our lives for more then a weekend a month and two weeks a year. By avoiding the real picture, I married my husband expecting the American Dream — 2.5 kids, house in the suburbs and dinner at 6 o'clock. The problem is that my ideal marriage did not involve my husband leaving for weeks or even months. My ideal marriage did not require me to deal with orders for him to go to war for a year.

If I had been honest from the start, I could have avoided the feelings of resentment I harbored for Rob and the Army. I would have had the clarity to realize that I married him despite the National Guard, and I would have to deal with the consequences of my decision.

This honesty leads to acceptance rather than resentment at the soldier's call to duty. Resentment is one of the biggest enemies of intimacy. By cutting out any fuel that might feed resentment a couple is able to avoid it. So how do you do that?

The first step is to clearly evaluate the decision you are making. Each step a couple takes in their journey allows for a choice to be made by each partner. This is true on all decisions -- whether to join the military or which movie to see. People all have different goals and hopes so a couple doesn't always agree on the path to pursue. This is where ultimatums often arise. Unfortunately, this is a sure-fire way to foster huge resentment. It was hard to do at first, but we had to eliminate "or else" from our discussions. That would be the first ground rule to set.

Next, it is important that each party get to express their desires and justifications. It should be done at a time when emotions are not heated. Pick a time when you are both prepared to have a discussion that allows for disagreements without attacking each other. Often, my husband and I would only discuss issues when we were mad about them. This got us nowhere. In order to truly be heard by your partner, you must truly listen to them. This is done by not thinking about counterarguments or what you are going to say next. A good rule-of-thumb is to explore your partner's argument with at least two questions before addressing your concerns. Then you are allowed to pay the same amount of attention to your views on the topic. This is the second ground rule: let each person completely express his or her choice and reasoning without interruption.

Now it is time for each of you to take a break and consider your partner's input. It often helps me to make a list of pros and cons that includes the points your partner brought up. This is the hard part. It is natural for people to hear what they want to hear instead of the facts. You might notice in considering your partner's points, that you decided what they said wasn't true or that it wasn't important. You may decide that some points should not be listed at all. It is important that you pay attention when you notice those thoughts because you could be denying or minimizing. In other words you could be lying to yourself.

Finally, you should discuss your decision with your partner. Differences of opinion should not be confused with ultimatums. I could have very well decided not to marry my husband because he was joining the National Guard. I would not have wanted him to change his mind because I was holding our future marriage hostage. I would have had to deal with his resentment. Basically, you have to decide how much you are willing to compromise and which alternative best achieves this. In my case, I decided to marry a man who could be sent to war. So as not to overly disrupt my life and career path, he decided to reduce his risk of deployment and join the National Guard instead of the active Army.

Being honest with yourself is a hard process because you are taking full responsibility for the ensuing repercussions. Sometimes the results are positive and sometimes they are not. When the outcome is painful, it is tempting to put the blame on someone else. For a very long time, I blamed my husband for leaving. Sometimes there is no blame. Sometimes bad things happen and we need to accept this and strive through it. This is where the second lesson comes in.

Lesson Two

When you are dishonest with yourself, you use blame as a mechanism for controlling what happens to you. This phenomenon can be seen in the criminal arena, especially with that of sex crimes. Many people blame the rape victim because of what she was wearing or how much she had to drink. What people fail to recognize is the truism that a lot of girls wear short skirts and a lot of girls get drunk. It is only when something goes wrong that those behaviors are considered aberrant. This tendency to blame the victim stems from a need to be in control of what happens to you. "The reason that horrible crime happened to that girl is because of something she did. I don't do those things so I will be fine."

The harsh reality is that we have no control whether some one will victimize us or not. In fact we have no control over what happens to us outside of our own behavior. Even the choices we make do not give us control over what happens next. My husband chose to join a unit that rarely gets activated, but that did not stop him from being transferred to a different unit that became part of the first group of National Guardsmen deployed for Operation Iraqi Freedom.

I had to learn to manage the fact that I could not choose my fate. Since I had not been honest with myself, it was a lot easier to be angry with my husband for joining the National Guard in the first place. It was his fault I was suffering and I could take it out on him. Luckily I had a month of pre-deployment preparation to deal with these issues, and I was able to talk on the phone with him on a semi regular basis while he was at Ft. Bliss. Eventually, I was able to realize the error of being deceitful with myself, and accept my fate – some of the time. Although there were periods when it was easier for me to regress to blaming my husband rather than accept responsibility for my part in the pain I was experiencing.

Usually, I was able to take responsibility for my actions, which meant changing my worldview. I went from being a confident person who believed that things were usually fair and if I worked hard enough, I could get what I wanted from life, to believing the complete opposite. I started to think that life was not fair, bad things happen to good people, and there is nothing I can do about it. This unhealthy way of thinking can lead to depression. Psychologist Martin Seligman (1998) calls this perspective learned helplessness. He describes it as "…a state of affairs in which nothing you choose to do affects what happens to you" (p.5). According to Seligman (1998), it is this type of thinking that leads people to give up on life and relinquish all control to fate. That means that you would intentionally pass on opportunities to bring yourself out of a painful state. It was vitally important that I shake off this hopelessness and learn to live with the circumstances I was given.

That is when I realized that I may not be able to control what others do or what happens to me, but I can control my response to it. The hard part is making that a reality. When my logical side recognized the most beneficial response to a situation, my heart was not always convinced. My heart would not let me get over the pain I was experiencing.

People commonly face this logic-emotion conflict on a day-to-day basis. Road rage is a good example of this: someone can cut you off in traffic, which is mildly annoying, but for some reason you feel like you are going to explode with anger. Logically, you know that what happened was not disastrous and no one got hurt, but when you are ruled by emotion you still feel like punching the guy in the face.

This is why I started living by a principle familiar to participants in the Alcoholics Anonymous Program: fake it 'til you make it. By acting the way your head tells you, eventually you will convince your heart to follow suit. So how does this apply to your loved one being deployed? Your heart may feel that you have lost all stability and control in your life, but if your head can come up with reasons to have hope, then listen. If you can't think of anything, I would recommend getting professional counseling.

Seeing a therapist during this time can be a very helpful way to gain perspective regarding your situation. Sometimes you feel like you can't talk to people about what is going on because they wouldn't understand or you don't want to bring them down. A therapist is the perfect person to release some of the fear, anxiety and sadness that you have built up. They also have the expertise necessary to determine if you are suffering from something serious, such as major depression. It is vitally important that you get help if you are having serious problems with depression.

Acceptance is the first step in learning how to live without your loved one. I am not saying that you will practice complete acceptance and understanding throughout the entire deployment process. It is a hard road to acceptance and your thought processes go through a variety of different evolutions. Dr. Elisabeth Kubler-Ross (1969) is most well-known for defining the stages of grief, which can help put some light on what you are going through. Her original studies observed people who were dying, and Kubler-Ross (1969), documented the mental state of her subjects as they came closer to death. Over time, her stages have been applied to a multitude of situations dealing with grief. In being separated from your loved one you are going through the stages of grief, and these stages are not sequential. You can always go back to a stage you thought you "got through". In the next chapter, these stages will be discussed in more detail. In order to support your husband before he leaves, you must accept the reality of his deployment.

I chose to sacrifice my "ideal" marriage so that my husband could join the Armed Forces. In my mind, this choice would benefit our relationship. I could not accept that my husband chose to sacrifice time with me, at the expense of our relationship, in order to benefit his career. It sounds a little twisted, but before 9/11 no one could foresee what would happen and the dramatic increase in deployments. I was not able to let go of the fact that he decided to risk leaving me, no matter how little that risk might have seemed at the time. I wasn't able to accept that part and it led to a distance between us.

Although this distance hurt us in the long run, it was helpful in the beginning.

My husband and I would fight about trivial things. We were both defensive and overly sensitive to one another's moods. In the end, these behaviors served to distance us from our emotions. It made his deployment a little easier. Not to sound insensitive, but when my husband left, I was glad to end to bickering. Sometimes, in order to be functional, you have to emotionally distance yourself from the situation. Although, it is important to realize that this is not a permanent solution. Eventually, your emotions will surface and they should be dealt with in a healthy manner.

I would recommend speaking with your family support group or a counselor. You would be better off if you did not handle your emotions alone. There are going to be many trials along this journey and it is not helpful to expend all of your emotional energy right now. Think of it like a bank account: if you overdraw on an account, you have to pay fees that end up costing you more. Letting others help you accept your emotions will conserve your emotional energy so you don't overdraw on your psychological checking account.

Family, friends, neighbors and co-workers all pitched in and did a lot to support me during this time. I received the most emotional support from other military wives, since I felt they understood what I was going through.

It is also helpful to start a journal to sort out the healthy and unhealthy ways you may be coping with the deployment. You may not be able to immediately identify your coping methods, but a week later when you read through your entries, patterns may arise and you may be spurred to break those patterns. I know that when I looked through my journal, I would find a lot of surprises about myself that I did not realize at the time. I also noticed large gaps of time when I did not write anything. I soon came to realize that the gaps in my journal signified the times I relied on unhealthy coping methods. I identified the times when I drank a lot of alcohol, because there was not a single entry during that period. I gradually came to realize that if I did not feel like writing in my journal that was a signal that I might not be coping very well. I was glad to have something I could refer to when I was lost or unsure about my emotional stability. Writing in my journal was a way to be honest with myself. Keeping yourself in check is very important; you are just beginning this journey and you are yet to say goodbye.

Saying Goodbye

෴

Saying goodbye is a hard stage. If you have had time to prepare for the deployment with your soldier, then you have developed routines and coping methods that are no longer effective. If you have not had time to prepare, then the difficult goodbye is complicated by other issues that cannot be discussed because your partner is already gone. I had to say good-bye twice: once in Flagstaff, AZ before they went to Ft. Bliss, and again at Ft. Bliss a month later. Each wife was determined to see their spouse as much as possible before deployment. Unfortunately, the two moments around Ft. Bliss were the only times we had. Looking back, I think it was better that way because there is something about saying goodbye that is so traumatic and wrenching.

The most energy-consuming aspect of saying goodbye is keeping a "stiff upper lip." Military wives have learned to do this for good reason; it is the best way to support your husband through this challenging time. I cannot begin to know how my husband felt at this time. I can only speculate that he shared the same fears and anxieties about our relationship as I did. By being strong, I was giving him the message that his home will not fall apart while he is away. I am sure he was doing the same for me. He seemed to have everything put together, and he did not seem overly worried about where he was headed. That really helped instill a lot of confidence in me. It was only fair that I return the favor.

I went with my husband to Flagstaff, AZ to prepare to deploy. I did not see him at all during the day because he was busy so I had to stay busy too. I did not want to be a mess by the time he got back to the hotel room. Besides, it was going to be our last few nights together for a long time. That is when I started reaching out to other military families. It helps you stay strong when you have a support system in place. No matter how emotional you are, the sooner you reach out to people the better. They will become the people you call at 2:00 am when you are worried sick because you haven't heard from your soldier.

The preparations eventually end, and it comes time to say goodbye. I was unlucky in the respect that my husband was part of the advanced party, so I was unable to witness the "big send off." I think it might have been more helpful to be part of the ceremony and feel the support of the families around me. I would have been able to watch the soldiers leave surrounded by others who felt my pain. I would not have been so alone. Instead we got up in the wee hours and I drove him to the base. I was flooded with so many emotions that I could not stop the tears from flowing. There was this sudden feeling of urgency - there was still so much to do, but we had run out of time. I had to fight every instinct to grab him and beg him not to get out of the car. But we had to say our goodbyes.

My husband said I could follow his car on the way to Ft. Bliss, since that was the direction I was headed. I was glad for that distraction because it allowed me to drive back to Phoenix without pulling over and crying. We stopped at a McDonald's, where I was able to keep a stiff upper lip and be strong in front of the other two soldiers that were with my husband. When it came time for me to leave the caravan and get off on my exit, I was numb once again. I decided that I needed to distract myself. I went into work in an attempt to keep that numb feeling that hid the pain I felt when he left. It was not until I got into the office that reality set in.

I remember walking through the doors at work that morning with great clarity. Everyone knew what happened to me, and my defenses started weakening when I noticed their stares. They looked at me with a mixture of pity, awkwardness, and fear of what to expect from me. One of my coworkers finally broke the silence and asked if I was okay. All I could do was shake my head, run to my office and close the door as the tears started pouring uncontrollably.

The comforting feeling of numbness was gone. Luckily, I work with a lot of concerned people who are used to dealing with people in crisis. I look back now and realize that going to work might have been a mistake. I was trying to run away from the emotions I was scared of but my body would not let me. I was able to work through it with some of my social work peers. It is important to reach out and get support when experiencing a shock like this.

The emotions you feel during the initial separation from your partner are not only scary for you, but also for those who care about you. You may notice that their reactions are strange or contrary to their normal behavior. It is hard to see someone in pain, especially if you love them. If your friends and family seem awkward, or do not know the "right way" to help you, feel free to tell them exactly what you need from them. Believe me, they will be relieved to know what they can do. By being candid about your needs and identifying whether a behavior is helpful or not, you can prevent any hard feelings from developing between yourself and your loved ones. You are still in a very weak state and blame can be very comforting. It is tempting to lash out at people trying to help you when they do something you find annoying or ineffective. I know that I was guilty of this a number of times.

Now that your soldier is gone, you are ready to face his absence. When the tears eventually stop, you're left wondering what you are supposed to do now. This is where you must find a way to continue on with your life. In order to maintain a functioning lifestyle, I had to come to terms with my husband's duty to his country and find a way to keep our home and our relationship alive. I also had to deal with the different phases of grief that I experienced.

The first stage in Elisabeth Kubler-Ross' five stages of grief has been discussed a lot up to this point: denial. According to Kubler-Ross (1969), denial acts as a "buffer" to allow a person to function and collect themselves before moving onto other coping mechanisms. She states that denial is often temporary and "will soon be replaced by partial acceptance" (p.53). As stated earlier, denial allowed me to prepare for my husband leaving. It also allowed me to celebrate my birthday with my friends two days after leaving Flagstaff, to continue my job of working with crime victims, and to keep my house clean. I could not stay in denial forever, and I soon came to realize that my husband was really gone and that I had to face it. I did not want to face it though and I did not think it was fair that I had to suffer my husband's absence while others did not.

Kubler-Ross' (1969) second stage is anger, and I found myself extremely angry with the powerlessness and loneliness I experienced throughout the entire deployment. This is the "why me stage". This anger can be randomly projected onto anything in your environment. I found myself angry at odd times about odd things. Once, I was mad that my neighbor's husband was allowed an early return from his deployment. I am not usually a jealous person, but my anger escalated to the point that I did not even want to talk with my neighbor. I also would get mad at complete strangers for saying harmless statements that I decided to take personally. Anger is a frustrating stage, and it distanced me tremendously from my support system because people did not like being around me very much. It also distanced me from my husband when I was angry at him for trivial reasons. I could not remain in the destructive, angry stage. I had to get control over my life.

That is where stage three came in. Kubler-Ross (1969) lists bargaining as the third stage. Most people bargain with God or some other higher power. I was no exception. I promised to go to Church every Sunday (which I rarely do) if my husband would just come home and ease my pain. I still wanted to believe there was some way I could control the situation. Since blaming people was alienating me from my friends, family and others who wanted to help, I thought bargaining might work. This reaction to grief may be the most private one since usually no one else knows that you have promised to do something in order to get your loved one home safely. With time, it becomes apparent that you have no control over your fate and bargaining no longer soothes you.

In fact there were times when nothing I did would soothe my pain. This leads to the fourth stage of depression (Kubler-Ross, 1969). As discussed in the last chapter, according to

Seligman (1998), helplessness can lead to depression. You can become depressed when you realize the ineffectiveness of your bargaining and admit your helplessness. According to Kubler-Ross (1969), this stage includes a "sense of great loss" and only those who have "been able to work through their anguish and anxieties are able to achieve this stage" (p.99-p.100). People often realize the benefits of therapy at this stage. I went to see a therapist because I am in the field and could recognize both symptoms of depression and substance abuse in myself. Some people get therapy because their friends and family suggest it after exhausting all efforts of being supportive. Regardless of the reason to seek help from a professional counselor, the important part is that you get help.

Some signs that you may be depressed include feeling down all the time, a disinterest in activity, and a lack of energy. You may also find that your eating habits and weight changes. This can be either weight gain or weight loss. Your sleeping could be drastically altered as well. You may be sleeping too much or too little. You may also feel worthless or even suicidal. When I help crime victims who exhibit these symptoms I get them into counseling immediately. I would suggest the same for you if this sounds familiar. It is also recommended that you see a psychiatrist for an evaluation for medication. People experience depression differently. For some, professional therapy provides the only relief; but for others, mild depression may be manageable with the help of their local support networks. Either way, it is important to work through your depression because it leads to the fifth stage.

The fifth stage, according to Dr. Kubler-Ross (1969), is acceptance. This is the hardest stage to achieve and often people are so stuck in their denial, anger or depression that they never get this far. According to Kubler-Ross (1969), once this stage is achieved it should not be considered a "happy stage". There is no magic lifting of mood because you accept what is happening to you. In reality, this stage involves letting go of the struggle with the inevitable, releasing pain, and maintaining a peaceful and dignified outlook on the present circumstances (p.124-p.125). There were few moments when I could say I found acceptance. It was a hard state to maintain in the chaotic military world, where new news could have sent me right back to denial in a heartbeat.

These stages are not meant to be something you achieve once and never have to deal with again. It is extremely common for people to fluctuate up and down through the list – including myself. Even though the stages of grief can seem endless, Kubler-Ross (1969), found that hope was a source of continuous comfort. Sometimes the only thing that helps us get through such trauma is the feeling that there is meaning and a reason behind our suffering. I found hope in loving my soldier, his job, and my country.

I found a lot of strength and comfort in becoming a patriot. I was able to get rid of my resentment and replace it with pride. I even went out and bought a bunch of patriotic music to listen to while I drove. Being patriotic helped alleviate some of the bad feelings I had toward my husband. It was important for me to deal with my emotional extremes on my own, because when I came home at the end of the day, there was no one with whom I could discuss my problems.

Living Alone

༶

Confiding in other people is one of the best survival tools for combating loneliness and abandonment. Effectively finding and employing a support network is no easy task. There are many personal obstacles to overcome in order to reach out to others; but, once you are able to, these friends, neighbors and family members become invaluable resources. However, overcoming those obstacles is easier said then done.

A major roadblock to reaching out to people is self-pity. I want to avoid the negative nature of this term, and instead, compare self-pity to an animal licking its wound. Like a wounded animal, you just want to be left alone.

You are in pain and have lost hope. All you want to do is wallow in your grief. This serves to preserve the connection to your loved one. There is a song by Dido called "Here With Me", which illustrates this concept. She describes the desire to keep her life with her loved one like a shrine for fear that she would forget what that life was like. Sometimes you feel obligated to mourn the temporary loss of your loved one. After all, how could you go on living as if he never affected your life?

You may experience the need to appear strong in front of other people because you don't want their pity. Military culture tries to cultivate this characteristic because the last thing a soldier wants to hear is a report from other people that their spouse is falling apart. You may think no one would be dense enough to say something like this but you would be surprised. The tendency to appear strong may lead you to behave stoically in front of those you trust and rely on. If you no longer let anyone know that you are suffering, you miss out on the support you so desperately need.

Disguising your pain is another obstacle that interferes with your ability to confide in other people. Your friends and family truly want to help ease your sorrow; however, when you care about someone it is hard to let them see you hurting. Sometimes they look at you with a helpless fear in their eyes and you are tempted to conceal your pain because you want that look to go away. If you appear to be in control, you can save your friends and family from any heartache, but the problem is that you are being strong for the people at home rather than your spouse. He is the one that needs your strength. You are not going to get the help you need by behaving in this manner.

The final roadblock is the lack of motivation and energy. This is a natural result of a depressed mood. The key to improving motivation and energy is to begin by taking small steps first. Instead of meeting your friends for a night out, you can send them an e-mail. Eventually you can move to bigger steps when you have developed your support network. Sometimes your friends and family can make it easier by coming to you. This is the best way to get your energy up because you don't have to expend much to get a recharge. Anyway you do it, it is important that you have the support in place for good and bad days.

I was fortunate to have friends that came to me. I had no idea how much I needed other people or how much they would help. The day after my husband left, I celebrated my birthday by canceling all previous plans so I could sit at home and cry. Moments after I got home from work, the doorbell rang. My friends brought dinner and cake and presents. They let me be sad when I needed to be sad, but they also cheered me up tremendously. I also had neighbors that reached out to me in the same way. They would often invite me to dinner or just hang out and talk, which helped me to not feel so alone.

The problem with being around other people when you are in such a sensitive state is that you can easily be upset or offended by what others say no matter how well intentioned it is. There are some common questions that spouses get about their deployed partner that are frustrating to answer.

"When is he coming home?" was the worst question for me. I was still trying to deal with the uncertainty of what was happening with my husband and every day, without fail, I would have to answer that stupid question. I hated telling people "I don't know," because it made me feel powerless and hopeless. Even worse, people who had already asked that question would say again, "Do you know when he is coming home yet?" It got so frustrating that I started snapping at these well-meaning people. Finally, I decided I would tell them to stop asking, because I would let them know if I got any news. That rationale seemed to work the best.

I soon realized that people ask those annoying questions as a means to show their concern, because they do not know what to say to you. In reality, there is probably not much anyone could say to make you feel better about the deployment. For me, the best discussions I had about my husband's deployment were those where the other person did not say much at all.

Other senseless, frustrating, annoying, irritating, bothersome, grating, maddening, etc. questions revolve around your opinions of the war, the president, the soldiers, and so on. I do not think people realized how personal and emotional those topics were to me. I realize now that they were curious to get my point of view, since I was so directly affected by the war in Iraq. Ironically, it is because I was so directly affected that I had such a hard time talking about these topics.

So how do you field all the frustrating questions coming your way? I started redirecting my anger at the situation onto the people asking me those painful questions. It did not make me a very pleasant person to be around. If I am not pleasant to be around, then I start to lose my support network. It became a self-destructive cycle that I had to break before I was completely alone again.

I accidentally stumbled onto the best way to handle those questions when one of my colleagues asked me yet again, "Do you know when he is coming home yet?" I decided to be honest, and I can't stress how effective honesty can be. I let him know that it hurts me every time someone brings that up, and that I would prefer for people to let me talk about it when I chose to. He never asked again, and in fact had a long discussion about fielding these types of inquiries, and it really helped me to deal with others asking me the same type of questions.

Naturally, those annoying questions are painful because you desperately want to know the answer. Unfortunately, as a byproduct of this desperation, I tortured my husband the same way I was tortured. Each time we communicated I would end up ask him at least one of those irritating questions (especially the one about him coming home). I quickly learned that communication with him was a completely different game then we were used to. We used to be able to be open about tough issues and work them out. Now I was faced with sporadic phone calls with strict time limits. There was not always adequate time to discuss tough issues. Besides, how cold I start a fight with my husband who could die tomorrow?

Whenever I got a letter or a phone call from my husband, it was bittersweet. I was ecstatic to hear from him but at the same time it brought back those lonely feelings I was hiding from. I found that we had developed a short hand to handle any household issues that I needed his input for. It was like a question answer session with no chitchat to interrupt. That way I could find out where to get our taxes done or what to do with his truck before time was up. I also liked to keep him informed of my decisions on household issues, in an effort to keep him connected.

It is important to talk about the mundane everyday situations because it is what keeps the connection. He needs to be connected to what home-life is like as much as possible. Most of us cannot imagine living in a country with a language and writing you can't understand and a populace you can't trust. Your husband has nothing that resembles home. Someone in that situation needs to hear about what things are like at home in order to feel connected and comforted. Getting minimal input is better than no input at all. It is going to be hard to adjust to having his input all the time when he gets home so it is best to keep your spouse involved as much as possible.

Keeping him involved also means making him aware of the emotions you are experiencing and listening to whatever feelings he chooses to express. This Sometimes requires you to communicate the unpleasant feelings you might have towards your husband. A lot of wives are scared to be angry with their loved one. They don't want to discuss disagreeable feelings in their weekly (if they're lucky) 10-minute phone call. The image of that phone call being your last is a haunting reality. You can't fight with your husband the last time you speak to him, so you don't discuss your difficult feelings at all. All of the "bad stuff" that occurs in real-life relationships is stored away instead of being dealt with. In addition to your relationship issues, there are other daily problems you must deal with while living alone. This is something a lot of spouses, including myself are not used to doing. In the end, wives have to develop a routine that accomplishes daily tasks without their husband's input. And so begins the gradual separation of the couple.

I stopped telling my husband about my little issues because they no longer seemed important in the big picture. I obsessed over how he was doing. I wanted to be able to comfort and support him since he was faced with his mortality on a daily basis. When we spoke on the phone, I was overly happy when I really wanted to cry. I did cry sometimes, but not often. I usually asked questions about how he was doing and reassured him that things were okay back home.

A few months into the deployment, I realized that I no longer felt close to my husband. I suddenly recognized that I acted so fake on the phone in an attempt to distance myself from him. It really bothered me. I wasn't sure how to handle the situation since I was not going to be able to talk with him on the phone any time soon. I decided the best I could do was write him a letter. Letters saved our marriage. I really didn't want to fight or bring him down over the phone, but I didn't want to be more disconnected than I had to.

Called to Duty

I had to develop a delicate compromise of letters and phone calls. At this time in your situation, it might be helpful to consult a therapist or a reputable self-help book on conflict resolution. This will ensure that your 10-minute conversation will not be filled with yelling and hurt feelings. Honesty is a good way to begin these conversations. Let him know that you are having a hard time and you want to talk about feelings that could be a little upsetting and difficult to articulate. Let him know that this conversation is necessary because you don't want to feel even more separated or distant than you already are. Let him know what is on your mind. Keep an eye on the clock, try to end the conversation with enough time to appropriately say goodbye. Before you hang up, reassure him that you love him and that you are glad that he is there for you. I was able to do this on the phone with my husband before he received the first letter that honestly expressed my emotions. I felt the need to give him some warning of what was coming in the mail. The fact that he would get the letter soon prevented me from being fake to him on the phone.

I am glad that I sent the letter. Some people feel good just writing it out, but I was trying to reconnect with my husband. Sending him the letter was the best way I could think of to let him into my world. In addition, I found that you can re-write letters and remove anything you don't mean or anything that would cause unintentional hurt. Letters allowed me to articulate my feelings without talking and saying something I really didn't mean in the heat of the moment. We talked about my letters once and he said he was glad to get them. He noticed the separation too. We had a phone conversation before he received the first letter. I was able to talk to him about the content of the letter that was on its way and, more importantly, I was able to get his input. He told me he wanted me to be real because that is what kept him connected to home. I did not realize I was hurting both of us by not being honest.

Sometimes this lack of honesty is unavoidable. I thought about the strong military wives in World War I and II, whose spouses would be gone for up to four years or more. They had no way to contact their husbands – no phones, no e-mail, and no R&R. There were times when I went months without hearing from my husband and it drove me crazy. I was determined not to watch the news because it usually sent me into a panic, but when I didn't hear form him I would sneak a peak every once in a while. I was desperate to hear that he was okay. It was irrational for me to be comforted that my husband's unit wasn't in the news since I would have known before the news organizations, but I had nowhere else to go for reassurance.

It wasn't until a few moths into the deployment that I realized no news is good news. Usually, it was only after traumatic events or close calls that soldiers made sure to call home. When they were doing okay the urgency to say, "I love you" one more time is not as great. I had to slowly and reluctantly accept the fact that if I heard nothing than nothing serious was going on. Daily life became easier when I relinquished my need to control a situation I had no control over. I stopped obsessing so much over his safety and the next time he would call. After that I could sleep a little better and concentrate at work.

It was during those times of silence that I truly felt alone. I lived home alone with out any children to take care of. It was just my cat and I, which is one of the most self-sufficient animals. After a few months my brother moved in, but he is a night owl that came home at four a.m. and slept all morning. I did not see him as much as you would expect. This is where I became in desperate need of my friends and family, more so than ever. The problem is that they were no longer able to meet my needs.

I know that a lot of my needs required more attention than was fair for my friends, but the lack of attention still hurt my feelings. I was bitter that I had to suffer like this and no one else did. I started to feel that I was entitled to large amounts of help and attention from my friends and family. This was satisfying for me at first, but their lives continued on while my stayed on pause. I was not allowed to move on with my life because if I would distance myself from my husband. At the same time people did not want to be around me if I was going to be such a downer. I was stuck. I was hurt. I was unable to be satisfied.

I felt a new level of helplessness when I confronted my new responsibility: I was expected to accept my husband's absence and move one without distancing myself from our relationship. The best example I can compare it to is being a teenager. Teenagers are expected to act and think like adults. They are praised by parents and teachers for being responsible and acting like adults; however, they are not always treated like adults. Teenagers are still controlled by the grown-ups in their lives. They are expected to burden the responsibilities of adults without being treated like adults. No wonder teens are so rebellious. No wonder I was so rebellious.

I thought I was going crazy. I found myself doing things I would not normally do and never have done before. Drinking became one of my most visible forms of rebellion. I started drinking almost everyday with my neighbors after work. My drinking escalated to the point where I had passed out more times than I had in my entire college career. The moment it became unmanageable was when I started blacking out and calling in to work because I was hung over.

I had sought counseling in the early stage of this rebellion. It would have been beneficial if my therapist had not tried to pry me out of my denial too early. I went for help and, just like a good therapist should, she saw immediately that my drinking was getting out of control. She decided to confront me and tell me to stop drinking without making sure I had other supports in place. She wanted me to remove socializing with my friends, my neighbors and even my father. I couldn't do it, so I stopped therapy. I wasn't ready for it then.

I continued the late-nights and the drinking. I hung out with anyone that was willing. I needed a big pool of people to draw from because everyone I spent time with could not do it every night. I still cannot figure out how I did it. I was so busy running from depression and grief that I did not notice my downward spiral.

My job saved me. It was a constant source of distraction through my husband's deployment process, and the organization's drastic changes allowed me less time to party. Right after my husband left, I found out that I might be laid off. Finances were not a big stress since my husband was able to support us, but I did not know what I would do without the job I enjoyed so much. Eventually, the organization found a way to budget, and I got to keep my job. It was reorganized though, and that is when I started to get my act together. I could not hide my behavior any more, and I wanted to keep my job.

Since I was virtually the only crisis worker assigned to the sex crimes unit, I could be called out at any time. This meant I had to remain sober. I was very concerned about making sure people thought I was doing well so as not to lose my job. I wanted to be available whenever needed so the drinking and the partying had to go. It was not an over-night process, but after realizing that I missed crisis calls because of my behavior, I decided to reprioritize my life.

Being good again was not as hard as I thought it would be. I decided to start working out and take up hobbies. I became a more well rounded person with lots of outlets for my emotions. I found that exercising was a great way to boost my mood even if I had to do it alone. I enjoyed making progress. I was able to go from running a mile everyday to running four. This is quite an accomplishment for someone who hates running. I was even able to find a pastime I could enjoy with my father that did not involve drinking. I started riding motocross with him on the weekends, which developed into a hobby I still enjoy.

Finally, I had developed a routine in my life alone. I was able to keep myself sane while staying connected to my husband and feeling the pain of his absence. Then I got the news that he would be coming home on leave and it sent me into chaos again.

Leave

☙

My husband called to tell me that he would be able to come home for two weeks. We were already seven months into the deployment and I thought that was the greatest news ever. I have since changed my mind but as the saying goes, hindsight is 20/20.

My first thought was, "the garage is a mess." The garage was so important because that was his room. I became obsessed with cleaning and organizing the house, but that is hard to do when you have an artist/brother living with you. Somehow my brother's oil paints had invaded almost every space of the garage. I was able to straighten it up but I made my brother scrub the paint off the floor.

My husband had many plans for how he was going to organize the garage, and he always took good care of it. I didn't want him to be upset about the condition it was in. I also didn't want him to be upset about any of the other changes in the house. Since he left I had decorated, painted, rearranged things, and got new furniture. He only had a month in our new house before he left and I wanted to make sure it still felt like home to him.

I also felt this overwhelming responsibility for handling our life and was afraid of being judged because of it. It goes back to the wife being put in charge of everything at home. A lot of military wives can become worried that their decisions won't measure up and that their husbands will be angry. My anxieties started with the upkeep of the house and the cars.

Luckily, my husband was home for only two weeks so I figured he would not have enough time to scrutinize everything. I tried to spend my time on the most important items and then get the rest as time permitted. Once I got myself motivated, I put the household in perfect

Called to Duty

order. I guess this is what expectant mothers experience in anticipation of their new baby. Although I was satisfied with my effort, I was exhausted. I promised myself I would start the preparations earlier when he came home for good.

Much to my relief, I had unconsciously been preparing myself for his homecoming. I had begun my reformation before I knew he was coming home so all of my rebel tendencies had disappeared. I would soon find out when he came home that I was ashamed of my earlier behavior. Had I not stopped those behaviors before his leave, I would not have enjoyed his visit so much. With my bad habits out of the way, I was able to prepare myself in other ways. Since I had been working out regularly, I was in better shape than when my husband left and I had been growing out my hair. I had to do my nails, style my hair and find the perfect outfit. I felt like I was a teenager again, getting ready for a date.

These preparations allowed me to ignore the stresses that had been plaguing me for the last seven months. It was nice to experience such a high when I hadn't for so long. While waiting for my husband to come home, I was filled with anticipation, like a child on Christmas Eve. It provided me a welcome respite from the anxiety I felt while he was in Iraq.

I had to fly to Maryland to meet him when he got to the States. I bought my ticket with a little help from my co-worker, despite the fact that I wasn't sure when or if he was actually coming home. Luckily my coworker had connections and got me a buddy pass from one of his friends. It allowed me to change flight times and dates if there was room on the plane. I also reserved a room in Maryland ahead of time, even though I wasn't sure when I really needed it. I didn't leave until I received a confirmation phone call one hour before my husband was boarding a plane in Kuwait – and then I was off.

I arrived in Baltimore, Maryland one night before my husband, so I had to sleep in the room alone. I was too excited to sleep. I got up and got ready way too early, so I had nothing to do in the hours before his plane arrived.

Called to Duty

I did not want to wait at the airport, so I sat in the hotel and played solitaire. When it was a decent hour I decided to try and call another wife who was in Baltimore to meet her husband. Silly me, I did not think any one else was like me. I was wrong. She had been ready for over an hour, and was resisting the urge to go to the airport as well. We decided to stop fighting the urge and meet each other there.

We swapped stories about our preparations and our trips to Maryland. They were remarkably similar which made me feel less crazy. I realized that I had some benefits over other wives, because money was not a real problem for me. I was able to take chances buying tickets and reserving rooms without worrying about the financial repercussions if plans had to be changed. The other wife I was with had to drive almost an hour away from the airport to find a room because she did not reserve one in advance. I just remember thinking how lucky I was not to have to do that.

As the hours passed we grew more anxious and giddy. It was finally time for the flight to arrive. We waited eagerly by the security checkpoint, which was as close as we could get to them. We looked intently at each shape that approached us. I felt like my heart was going to leap out of my chest. Repeatedly we were told by the security lady to back up because we kept inching forward to get a better look. When I finally saw him there was no way that security lady was going to keep me away from him; and once they learned whom we were waiting for, the surrounding people wouldn't let her either. Immediately, I ran into his arms. It was hard to say anything at all. All I could do was hold him to make sure he was real. Then I looked at him and he was so different. He had changed drastically; probably due to the limited food and heavy workloads he had to endure. It threw me off balance a little bit. At least his smile was still the same.

We arose from the fog and proceeded to try to act normal. We went to get his baggage and had the usual small talk: "How was your flight?", "Did you wait long?", "Are you hungry?" - I wasn't sure what else to say. How do you

Called to Duty

talk to a person you haven't been able to talk meaningfully with in seven months? I forgot how to have a long conversation. I was used to compacting all we had to say to each into other ten or fifteen minutes. Since we were both so tired when we got to the hotel, we did not talk much and went right to bed. We slept so soundly in each other's arms. It was the best sleep either of us had since he left. When we woke up, talking was not a problem anymore. He was back.

During his visit, we were alone for only a short time. I had long been worrying about the logistics of his visit home. I was worried about having to share him with everyone else. I felt so selfish. After all, his parents had been part of his life a lot longer than I had. I could not help thinking that I was entitled to have him all to myself. I used to revel in daydreams, in which I told everyone that he simply did not have time to visit with them; however, had I fulfilled this selfish wish, I would have been disrespecting the needs of his friends and family. I am sure he wanted to see his mom and dad as well as me after being gone for so long.

This is a normal reaction for most spouses when their loved ones come home on leave. But it is best to share him with everyone. Your kindergarten teacher was right when she taught you to share. It is important that your spouse get to see their family for many reasons. In my own experience family and friends had been really supportive of me while he was gone and deserved to see him. He deserved to see whomever he wanted, and I did not feel like a very good person hogging him all to myself. In the end, I didn't have to worry because sharing my husband ended up being beneficial to us both.

We spent a day touring Washington D.C. and getting used to each other. His mother joined us since she lived in Virginia. It was nice to be distracted by someone else's conversation, since it was hard for us to fill up the quiet times. There were a lot of things we did not want to discuss with each other. Difficult issues and hard feelings that might have caused tension or pain had no place in this two-week break.

Called to Duty

When we got back to Phoenix, we had the grand-plan of getting our entire family together for one evening, so we could spend the rest of his visit alone together. Everyone met at a local restaurant that is well equipped for large gathering such as ours. We mingled with all of our loved ones, shared emotional toasts, and my husband told some of his war stories. It was a wonderful night and my husband gave a very sweet toast about how he could not do his duty overseas without my support.

For the last two days of his visit home, my husband and I were able to spend it however we wished. We developed a pattern during that time, wherein we would spend time alone, but not enough to start talking about serious issues. We would sidestep those conversations by finding old friends to visit with. We even went so far as to look up some of the people from his old National Guard Unit at the armory. I never thought I would have ended up there. I had fantasies of a romantic two weeks together, but when it came down to it, I didn't feel like it and neither did he.

In the end, we had a great time together so long as we kept ourselves distracted from reality. My favorite coping mechanism of all time, denial, saved the day. Eventually, I had to emerge from my fantasyland and say goodbye… again.

We went to the airport together and I parked in order to spend an extra ten minutes with him. He was going back to Maryland a day early to avoid any travel problems that might prevent him from reporting on time. In my head that was a smart move, but my heart was screaming for him to stay one more day. I could tell he was torn too, but he kept that strong face and used his sense of humor to cover up what was really going on. I remember walking from the ticket counter to the x-ray machines with him. My feet felt so heavy and my head was really foggy. I knew there were a lot of people around me, but it felt like the airport was deserted.

We stood holding each other for what felt like forever until we both knew he had to go through the checkpoint. Tears were already streaming down my face as I silently

Called to Duty

watched him walk away. I was frozen with grief, but I wanted to buy a ticket to Maryland and spend his one last day together. After he cleared through the checkpoint, I watched until I could not see him anymore. Then I started to sob. I sat with a ripped piece of toilet paper from the airport bathroom and cried uncontrollably. There was no way I could leave the airport. I could not even pull myself together enough to walk to my car. It was then that I noticed all the people around me. There was a couple kissing each other goodbye and a family trying to corral their kids. I remember an older couple playing happily with their grandchild. I looked in vain to make a connection with any human being to help me with this pain. I wanted so badly for someone to approach me and ask if they could help, but I don't know what I would have said if they did. I just wanted it to happen. In the twenty minutes of my sobbing not a single person would even look my way. I felt so abandoned and helpless.

I finally got up, walked out of the airport and drove home. I felt exactly the same as when I had to leave my husband the first time. The only difference was that I knew how

I was going to feel for the next few days and weeks. I already knew what was in store for me…sort of.

My husband, having already spent seven months in Iraq, had figured out what was essential and what was not out of the gear he brought with him. He decided to bring all non-essential items back to Phoenix, to make it easier to pack when he came home. When I saw all of his things strewn across the floor, I broke down again. I decided to do the laundry, but I was overcome with hopelessness. I thought to myself, "What is the point of washing these jeans or this shirt? He won't be home anytime soon to wear it anyway."

My stages of grief resurfaced, and cycled over and over again. Some how I had to resume the routine I had developed when he left the first time; however, those methods were not working, and the holidays were approaching.

Holidays are challenging for everyone, and they are especially rough on people who are dealing with depression, grief, or loss. I was trying to get my life back on track at the most chaotic time of the year. The first step I took toward feeling better was to throw myself back into work. If I was having a hard time with the holidays, then the victims I was helping were too. Work served as a good tool to perpetuate my denial, but depression was starting to intrude on my life.

When the holidays finally rolled around, I visited our families as if my husband were home. I made sure to make time for my in-laws as well as my own family. I felt obligated. Otherwise I might have avoided my in-laws in order to remain in denial. Each time I saw them, it was a painful process because it emphasized my husband's absence. I had never spent time with my in-laws without him. They always wanted to hear stories about what he was doing and how he was feeling. I couldn't get away from his "absence" for a second. It was not as bad going to my family's house though.

While spending the holidays with my family, I was able to revert back to my little girl self that was not married to anyone. As usual, they asked how he was doing, and I got the sympathy, but it was not nearly as bad. It was helpful to me to return to a place where I was used to being without my husband. That was why my Grandmother's house was such a haven for me. Even though I held onto my cell phone for dear life and made sure to mail him a letter every day, I was able to get back into my comfy little denial zone and surround myself in the warmth of Grandma's kitchen.

After the holidays I was still trying to return to the comfortable routine I had developed before my husband's leave, but it was not happening. All of the good coping mechanisms I had learned before he came home on leave were not working this time. I had to reorganize my life while preparing for his return home since his orders might be up at the end of February. It was time to prepare for his homecoming, but first I had to get through yet another birthday and Valentine's Day without him.

He's Coming Home

☙

He was supposed to be gone for one year. That was what we were told, but any experienced National Guard Soldier's wife knows not to trust those deceptive orders. I expected him to miss my birthday by a few days because it might take some time to out process. I was not expecting him to miss it by a few months.

How do you prepare for a homecoming when the date is constantly changing? You nest. Nesting is a wonderful way to feel like you have some control over an aspect of your life that you really do not. Mother's know what I am talking about. They have a natural instinct to prepare for baby and make sure everything is perfect before he/she is born, such as, painting the nursery, getting the furniture, having all of the outfits clean and ready, and setting out the diapers and wipes. I did much the same thing. I decided I had to do a major spring-cleaning of the entire house, which actually took up a lot of my time. I made sure his garage was in order and the way he liked it. I made sure his clothes were clean and hanging in the closet. I also thought I should buy him a few new things to wear.

I also decided to prepare the backyard for his arrival. We had agreed that I would leave it unlandscaped so that he could have some input in our new house. There was an abundance of weeds and rocks that would make landscaping extremely hard, so I decided to remove it all. I raked up all the rocks and dumped them, pile by pile, into the garbage each week. It was not until later that I realized that I did not need to remove rocks from our yard. I had a compulsion to make everything clean. It was an obsession for me. I think I was trying to control my life and keep my mind off of the chaos. Not knowing when he would come home was driving me crazy.

This nesting behavior in its many forms continued up to the day he walked in the door and for some time afterwards. It developed into yet another tool to cope with an unpredictable life. While I was clearing out the house and making it ready for the homecoming, I had to do the same with myself. I had to come to terms with the fact that I had evolved into a different person than the one my husband left behind. There were positives and negatives to this exploration.

I found it helpful to work with a therapist before he came home. She helped me deal with the negatives and discover the positives about myself that had developed throughout the deployment. One of the major negatives I had to work through was the loss of my favorite coping mechanism, denial. Without denial, I was forced to face all the ugly things I was feeling about my husband, my country, and myself. It was useful to push those things away when there was nothing I could do about my situation, but it was not useful anymore. There was no way I was going to keep a lid on those negative emotions; I had to get them out.

The first repressed emotion I chose to deal with was abandonment. Despite the fact that my husband had no choice, I still felt like he deserted me. The idea was irrational, but I could not remove the feeling from my heart. I had to confront that issue in order to put my heart and my head in the same place. A lot of my problems stemmed from experiences I had in my past, which is so often the case with people dealing with abandonment. I could not dismiss the feeling that he deliberately joined the National Guard, knowing that he would leave me. I wanted to be able to blame him for the pain I felt because he was both an easy and safe target. He was an easy outlet because he was the one who left. He was safe because I could direct my irrational emotions his way since he was thousands of miles away and would never know - or so I thought. In reality, he would eventually come to know. I knew this deep inside and I worked with the counselor on how to discuss my feelings of abandonment with my husband.

I also had a secret indignation against the government and the military for taking him away. My public face was always supportive of the military and the government. I

Called to Duty

could not bear for anyone to think that I did not approve of my husband's presence in Iraq. The truth is that I supported my husband while he was deployed, and I was not against the War in Iraq, as so many assumed I would be. I was angry at the military, but that resentment was irrational. Deep down I knew that he signed up for a job and the military was requesting that he do it. I was still mad because they took my husband from me. Some of my anger was justified because they constantly changed his orders and duties. Eventually, I was able to focus my frustration with the U.S. military onto the issues that really counted such as pay or extension of orders. It also allowed me to direct the majority of my negative emotion away from my husband and towards the disappointment I found within the military structure.

I was often tempted to take action. Sometimes I felt like taking my complaints up the chain to Arizona Senator John McCain, but I never did. I had to accept that some people are called on to make greater sacrifices for others. He chose to do this and I chose to marry him. If I really felt that we were being mistreated, I would have done something. But the U.S. military did not violate any laws or rights. What they did was emotionally unbearable, but not illegal or inhumane (but pretty close). Even those feelings I had toward the military began to subside the more I acknowledged and talked through them.

Finally after dealing with all of the emotions and anger directed at other things I had to acknowledge that I was disappointed and disgusted with myself. I was disappointed in myself for having those harsh feelings towards my husband and my country. I was disappointed that I was not a more supportive wife. I was sad that I could not be stronger and make sure my husband did not worry about me at home. I was disappointed that I could not handle this thing by myself and I was embarrassed that I needed so many people to help me. I was also angry with myself for not treating those who helped me better. I had a lot of things I wanted to beat myself up over.

That brings me to the second negative feeling I had to work with, self-pity. I was extremely wrapped up in what I was going through and what I felt. I had to expand my awareness of the world to experiences outside of myself, starting with my husband. This also aided me in letting go of the anger I felt towards him. My therapist helped me realize that all my changes, emotions, and struggles corresponded with his. She helped me get outside of my head and garner sympathy. In trying to become strong enough to make it through a military deployment I lost my ability to sympathize. This is ironic since I was a crisis counselor. Looking back on my work, I realized that most of my victims were helped by an empty shell that knew all the right things to say because of years of practice, not because of understanding and empathy.

When I came out of my self-pity party, I felt more pain but I was also able to feel more of everything else. People started talking to me more because they enjoyed it and not out of sympathy for my situation. Conversations with my husband were better. He was still unable to discuss the details of what he was going through, but I felt more comfortable listening to what he felt and exploring that. He relied on me to bring it out of him, as he always has. By interacting with my husband the way I used to, he felt more comfortable talking and we began to make the connection I thought we'd lost months ago.

When I stopped feeling sorry for myself, I could see the ways I had grown from this experience. It was then that I could deal with the positive aspects of myself. The most important was my newfound independence. I had never lived alone. I went from my family to college roommates to my husband. I was rarely ever home alone. Even when my husband went to boot camp, I was living with two other girls so I was never left totally by myself. While my brother did live with me for some months, I was still able to live alone for that majority of a year which I never would have imagined possible. I found that I had plenty of things I enjoyed doing on my own. I also learned that I was very capable of taking care of things by myself. I was able to hire a contractor for a very good price and get a building permit for our patio. I was able to move a queen-sized sleeper sofa by myself, which required the removal of a door and an intricate pulley system that I developed using bungee cords and tie-downs.

Along the same lines, I discovered that I was not as dependent on my marital relationship. I had an unhealthy reliance on my husband that often interfered with both of our lives. I deferred spending time with my friends in order to be with my husband, and I expected him to do the same. Needless to say this did not work well with my husband since he naturally wanted to do things with his friends every once in a while. My friends also missed me. After being without my husband for so long, I shook off that dependence. I realized how much fuller life could be if I lived mine and he lived his.

As homecoming neared, I discovered what a strong person I was and that my relationship with my husband was strong as well. It got easier to look back and see how far I came when there was an end in sight. When I had no idea when my husband would return, it was too hard to look back at how far I had come because I had no idea how far I had left to go. When I was ready to see my strength I was able to use that strength to overcome the remaining emotional obstacles left before and after my husband came home.

As homecoming time got closer, I could not contain my excitement. I drove down to El Paso, Texas where he would be flying in. Other military wives were staying in the same hotel as me, waiting anxiously for their husbands. We all went shopping to make sure we had the perfect outfits and that our hubbies had civvies to wear when they got to spend the weekend with us after landing. We also had to do something with our nervous energy. We walked up and down the mall several times and went to the PX to get snacks that our husbands might be craving. All the while we kept our phones near and each time one of us received new news about the arrival it would pass through the grapevine. Finally I received a call from my husband saying he was stateside and would be home in three hours. I rushed to tell the Captain's wife, who was shopping with me. We called the others to let them know, purchased the finishing touches for our outfits, and got back to the hotel to shower and get ready.

It usually takes forever for me to get ready for something special. This time it took no time at all. I went down the hall to see if the Captain's wife had rushed as well. We both had the same predicament, which happened to be the story of our entire year: we got ready too early, and now there was nothing to do but wait. We thought we would go early to scope out the place where we would finally see our husbands. We got there only to find out that we weren't the only ones with that idea. Plenty of people could not wait to get there and…wait for hours. As with any airline, there were delays and other issues that led to the plane arriving hours later. We all waited inside, believing we had to, until some brave sole ventured out towards the runway. That opened the floodgates to a hoard of families lining up as far as they would let us near the runway to wait. It was incredibly windy. I remember thinking how hard I had worked to get my hair just right and now it doesn't matter anymore. Then I thought, "What is he going to care about my hair anyway?" I am sure he wants to see me just as much as I want to see him. It is silly what we think of sometimes.

The band started marching down the runway and that signaled to us how close our husband's were. We saw some lights far off coming our way. The plane finally arrived. It was as if it were moving through molasses. The plane never seemed to get closer. It felt like hours before the plane was close enough to even be recognized. When it landed it started to register in my mind that my husband was finally home safe. Relief washed over me and was soon replaced by annoyance because they were not getting off the plane. It took them more than fifteen minutes to even open the door.

I expected that the homecoming would be like the ones you see on television, with the husband rushing to his family with his bag slung on his back. His family would be running towards the plane with banners or flowers and they would meet in the middle embracing each other with their eyes shut tight so no tears would escape. That was not quite what happened. We were restricted behind a rope barrier and had to watch in agony while they marched past us and into the building. We all started to run into the building after we realized we could not see the person for whom we were waiting. Once inside, we had to stay behind another barrier while they stood in formation in front of us. The tension was incredible on both sides. There were two groups of people within twenty feet of each other, aching to be with someone they have not seen in a year. Our soldiers were finally home from a place they would just as soon forget. At this time, the Army thought it would be a great idea to have a high-ranking official give a speech. That just fueled my already healthy distaste for the military. They had our husbands for over a year, what is it going to hurt to have them be with families instead of hearing an "atta-boy" speech from someone they have never met?

Suddenly, it happened. I could not hear the speech since there were no microphones, but I could hear the captain yell some phrase that sent the soldiers flying in our direction. I was in a panic because I could not find him anywhere. He found me though. He had been coming straight for me when I finally saw him. Finally the television scene occurred. We came rushing towards each other. I saw his face long enough to see that it was tearing up, and then we held each other with our eyes squeezed shut. Finally I had to let go because I wanted to see his face. What do you say in that moment to sum up everything you are feeling? I couldn't think of anything but my husband did. He simply said, "I missed you so much". That is what it came down to. This whole time, everything I was experiencing was the complicated process of missing someone so vital to my life. I was lucky. My missing was over. Some soldiers never came home and some wives never got to feel what I felt at that moment.

After all this rush of emotion they made the soldiers return to their ranks, get on some busses and do a bunch of bureaucratic stuff, while we wives waited around for them to finish. We were all so silly, frantically following the busses in our cars. We all were diverted because we were not allowed to follow the busses through a certain area of the base. There were a lot of women that became panicked and demanding when that happened; however, some of us were able to keep it together, listen to the poor MP, and get the directions to the place where we could meet up with our men once they were finished.

We waited once again for what felt like an eternity. Finally, I saw my man coming towards my parked car with his bags in his hands. He got in the car and was so tired he could only think about sleeping by my side again. I was so grateful to have him back that I didn't even poke him when he started snoring as he slept beside me. The next morning we realized we only had a day together before he had to get back to work again. We did our normal stuff; movies, eating out, window-shopping. We picked up right where we left off. At least it seemed as if we did.

Although he had to go back to work, we were allowed to stay the night together at the hotel in El Paso. I was able to work out in the gym and lounge around the pool, and finally have my husband back at night. We tried to get his cell phone working so I could communicate with him, but it could not be programmed. We bought him a new phone because his old one was broken. The whole process was such a foreign experience to me, since I was not able to freely communicate with him in months. I was so excited at the prospect of calling him when I needed to. Sprint said that it would take up to six hours to have his phone working with his old number again, but that didn't work. A couple of days went by and the phone still did not work, which sent me into a sudden and completely irrational panic.

I had just spent the majority of the fourteen months he was gone in a communication dead-zone and I was going crazy with the reality that I wouldn't hear from him until he came back to the hotel. I was also egged-on by the fact that other women were able to communicate with their husbands and to make arrangements to meet them for lunch and during other breaks. I was fuming because I could not do the same. There was one time that the Captain's wife asked her husband to stay with mine because we were going to come there together to eat lunch with them. But when I got there, my husband was not. The Captain, anxious to spend time with his wife, told me I could probably catch him at the dining facility. I got directions, went over there and walked through the entire facility. I thought I saw him two separate times and embarrassed myself once by almost touching a stranger on his back mistaking him for my husband. He wasn't there. I became dejected and gave up. It was a horrible experience.

Called to Duty

Naturally, I took out my emotional turmoil on the customer service representative at Sprint. It was the oddest thing I have ever done. I broke down crying to the Sprint lady telling her about why it was so vital that my husband's phone works immediately. Thankfully, she decided to help me despite how crazy I sounded. She gave him a temporary number until the whole mess got figured out. I was so happy to hear that. I was worried that once I left him behind in El Paso I wouldn't be able to talk to him again.

Now I realize that some of those feelings were residuals from feeling abandoned by my husband and having him ripped out of my life. That was the first taste of the feelings that would haunt me throughout our reunification process. Eventually I did have to leave him again. I had to go back to work and he had to start staying on the base. I went home and continued my nesting habits until I was to go to Flagstaff and see my husband parade down the street and into the armory where he would be officially home.

There was yet another period of waiting for my husband to arrive at an undisclosed time. There was no word on how long it would take the soldiers to out-process and come back from El Paso. Then the day arrived for the soldiers to return to Flagstaff, AZ. The busses finally showed and some of the soldiers had climbed through the roof of the bus and sat on the top. I could see my husband sitting on top of the second bus. I yelled and yelled to get his attention but I couldn't. I rushed inside to stand right by the doors where they would walk in. He ended up standing at attention right in front of me. That was good because this time I would be able to find him right away. The military had to do their pomp and circumstance once again. There were numerous speeches all of which took way too long. I couldn't help thinking that this was all a waste since not a single person in the room was interested in what any of the speakers had to say. Finally, we were free to go, again.

It was a surreal experience leaving the Flagstaff armory. I remember the first time I was in that place and how foreign the whole experience felt to me. Now here we were

Called to Duty

again, only this time both my husband and I knew people to talk with; but the people I knew were different from his friends. He was saying goodbye to men he had developed friendships with that I had never seen before. I was saying goodbye to women I had grown to trust that he had never met before. It was as if we had this entire intimate life apart from each other. I never thought that would have been possible. After the goodbyes, we headed to the little motel the military provided for us to stay in because, of course, he still had more out-processing to do.

We came home to our friends and family eagerly awaiting our arrival. I had arranged for everyone to surprise my husband by being there when we got home. I think the large number of cars lined up outside clued him in on what was going on. He also saw his father outside of the house getting something from his car. It was a pretty emotional moment to see them hug each other. We walked inside and my husband got to hug everyone, we ate lots of food and my husband told lots of stories for everyone to know a small view of what he has been up to for the last year. We looked at pictures and our family cleaned everything up so we didn't have to. It was a really great time and we were fortunate to enjoy it while we were still in our honeymoon period.

When the dust settled and we were home alone together, things became a little touchy. I think we both had our own issues and insecurities that we were trying to deal with and we started taking it out on each other. It all started with our vacation time, which involved our grand plans for his homecoming.

He was going to whisk me away somewhere romantic and fun to spend time together as soon as he got back. We decided that we should do it that way so he did not have to worry about taking time off from work. I had millions of fantasies involving beaches, amusement parks, cabins… there were so many places I could think of where we could have gone. Then he came home. Reality set in and he realized he didn't feel like leaving home. Even worse, he didn't feel like spending time with me. I had taken some vacation time off from work to spend time with him, but he told me that I should go back to work. I was confused and hurt and refused to go back. I'll be damned if I was going to leave him at home alone, just as soon as he came back into my life. I just didn't understand.

The only thing I accomplished by staying at home was to seal the official death of our honeymoon period. It was a pretty rocky time, where we wasted most of our time together fighting. He didn't feel like he was in his own home because there had been so many changes. I didn't feel like he still loved me because he wanted to be left alone all the time. He felt like I didn't care about what he went through, while I felt like he didn't care about what I had to deal with. Plus, I never got my vacation. That was what I concentrated all of my resentment on. It was something easy to conceptualize and completely his fault so I decided to use that problem as the scapegoat for all the issues we had festering under the surface.

We were having a serious communication breakdown. The more he withdrew the more I was mad. I could not identify exactly why I was mad at him, so I picked other problems to take out my aggression on him. The more

I attacked him the more he withdrew. You can see how this can't lead to anything good.

During communication breakdowns, both parties often act out some unhealthy behaviors in order to feel like they have been heard. My husband chose a behavior he was very good at: retreating. By refusing to deal with a person or problem, the retreator feels a sense of control over the situation because he or she is able to decide whether or not to confront the problem. The retreator decides when an issue will be dealt with, and there is no telling when that time will be.

This is an extremely frustrating behavior for whoever is on the receiving end. This leads to another unhealthy behavior, nagging. This was something I was good at. If the nagger's opinions are not acknowledged, he or she will keep repeating the message until the nagger gets recognized. In this case, the nagger feels in control because he or she will not accept being ignored. The only thing that can stop the nagger is if you physically leave.

Called to Duty

This leads to another unhealthy behavior, leaving. Like the retreator, the leaver will not deal with a person or problem. The leaver physically removes him/herself from the situation and cuts off all methods of communication. This is most commonly done in response to being on the receiving end of a nagger. Naturally, this is the technique that bothered me the most because I already had a lot of issues surrounding abandonment. The leaver takes control of the situation by ending the communication only to be resumed upon their return.

Sometimes when someone feels utterly powerless because of these tactics, then they will retaliate with a subversive technique, martyrdom. It is extremely hard to detect when someone is playing the martyr role unless they do it a lot. This is because the martyr makes you feel like you did something so wrong and hurtful so that you feel guilty. Sometimes the hurt is real and sometimes not, but the martyr has gained the upper hand by ignoring any pain you may have had inflicted on you and forcing you to deal with their pain by blaming you.

Another behavior that impedes communication is bullying. While all of the previous behaviors are unhealthy, this is one of the more dangerous ones because it can lead to violence. That is the most extreme situation. Bullies can call names, belittle, break items, yell, use intimidating postures and finally use physical violence. It is important that if someone is dealing with a bully, they need to get help and find a safe place to stay. The bully needs to get help in order to control their feelings before the relationship can safely be resumed.

Now that the unhealthy behavior patterns resulting from poor communication have been discussed, what can be done about them? My husband and I took a long time admitting that we could not break some of these patterns and that we needed some professional help. After a few sessions, we were able to take what we had learned and apply it to all of our issues with each other. It comes down to respecting, listening and talking to your partner.

Respecting your partner involves accepting your partner the way they are and realizing that they may handle things

Called to Duty

differently then you. I was the type of person that liked to work through a problem until it was solved no matter what grueling process that entailed. My husband liked to have time to alone to calm down a bit before continuing when things got too heated. These two approaches did not mesh well together. We both had to work together for a compromise. He realized he could not leave every time something got uncomfortable, and I realized that I had to accept that there were some times when he should be alone. When you let the other person know what you need, it is easier to understand and respect you partner's needs and wishes.

In order to respect your partner's needs and wishes you need to listen. Often when people are arguing they are so concerned about getting their point across that they form their rebuttal while their partner is still talking. It takes a lot of practice but by simply acknowledging what your partner said, you have shown that you are listening. It is also important that if you get it wrong, you allow your spouse to correct your perceptions. It is amazing how out-of-hand an argument can get because people misunderstand the intentions of the other person. Listening prevents this from happening.

After you have listened to your partner, it is important that he or she listens to you. It is a lot easier for your angry partner to hear you when you present your message in a non-threatening manner. When I help couples communicate through my work with the police department, I have them use statements like: "I want…" or "I need…" This allows them to communicate their needs clearly to each other without blame. When I had problems with my husband leaving during heated arguments, I used to say "Go ahead and leave, you always leave and you don't care about us." I eventually realized that I was not using the techniques I have taught my clients. Upon this realization, I rephrased my statement and said, "I need you to stick around because when you don't, I feel abandoned and unloved."

It is amazing how calming a phrase like that can be. Suddenly, the person you are talking to realizes that you are just as wrapped up in the issue as they are. By not accusing them of anything, you are allowing them to respond to you without being defensive. It is important when talking with your partner that you speak honestly and avoid any type of insulting or disrespectful remarks. Those only allow the argument to grow. As stated before, you may need to get some outside help from a counselor to get to this point. With a little practice my husband and I realized we were having a lot less arguments. We were able to stop arguments before they started.

Getting to that point was a long process and a lot of work. I had many issues to deal with and so did he. Those issues were things that we needed to figure out on our own, but that didn't mean I left my husband to his own devices. I was very supportive of him when he needed me. I was able to listen when he wanted to talk and left him alone when he needed it. I encouraged him when he was feeling down, and he did all these things for me. We both had to realize that it was not our jobs to fix one another. Once we got past that, it was a lot easier for me to accept the times my husband wanted to spend time alone.

My husband learned to accept the motorcycle I had bought while he was gone. At first he seemed a little bitter that I spent so much of our money on a toy for me. Even though I was perfectly capable and willing to share, he saw better uses for the money and was not all that interested in the motorcycle anyway. It wasn't until he realized that riding the bike is what helped me cope with the extreme stress I experienced during his deployment, that he came to appreciate the motorcycle. Soon I too came to appreciate his hobby, hunting, even though I don't care for it.

During this entire process of push and pull and give and take we were slowly realizing the changes that we went through apart from each other. Our core selves were still intact. I could count on my husband choosing to clean the entire house before undertaking a task he was not looking forward to. He could count on me doing my crossword puzzle after work before doing anything else. We were still ourselves but we weren't.

Being alone gave me a chance to reflect on what I would like to change about myself and forced me to change

Called to Duty

things I did not want to change. We had to get to know each other all over again. This experience can be exciting, in that it is nice to be surprised by your spouse's behavior when you have been with them for so long. It is also nice to be proud of how far you have come and to want to share this with your partner. The only problem is the preconceived notions that we had developed about one another. We kept expecting and assuming things about each other that just weren't true any more.

We are still trying to work through those expectations. It is hard to treat a person you have been with for so long as if you hadn't known them; however, that is what we needed to do in order to know the new person we each had become.

During the chaotic process of improving our communication, working on our own issues, and getting to know each other again, we also realized that the way we had lived our lives for the past year had to end. This is especially hard for the spouse who stayed home. In my case, my husband had only lived in our home for one month before he left. The home he returned to was very much my own. That was a big problem between us.

I had everything arranged the way I wanted it to be arranged. I painted the rooms the way I wanted them painted. I had my own systems to keep the house clean, pay the bills, and even get ready in the morning. I had the television shows I watched at night, and I had a dinner routine that did not involve any real meals. It was extremely hard for me to let all of this go. I had relied on these routines for so long to get me through the day. I could not just throw them out. They were developed as a way to cope with chaos. As far as I was concerned, the chaos was not over just because he was home. He was, after all, still in the National Guard. I have learned not to turn my back on that Organization. They sneak up on you and do things to your life that you never thought possible, all the while telling you they would never do anything like that.

My husband was more than happy to give up his routines, being that they involved living in intolerable climates

Called to Duty

without indoor plumbing. He was also anxious to make his mark on the house since he did not have the chance before he left. This was a problem for me. Every time he touched something that I had taken care of while he was gone, I got extremely offended. Even the order in which the housework was done bugged me when he got involved. I also took it personally. I thought he was criticizing the way I had handled things while he was gone. I was already very self-conscious about that in the first place, but to have him come in and change things was like a slap in the face. When we learned to better communicate with each other, we were able to work through my fears of inadequacy and develop a compromise on some of my "systems".

Because he started changing things around and the life I knew was not running so smoothly anymore, there was the inevitable late-payment-problem. I had an elaborate system of bills and mail on the entryway table that he had not yet learned and, of course, a bill did not get paid on time. I *knew* the reason was that he put the mail in the wrong place and I had no idea we even had that bill.

I was right, but I also used that as ammunition to prove that my way worked and his did not. That was not a very productive way to proceed with things. By taking that stance, I prolonged an argument for over a week when I could have just asked him to leave the mail for me to sort in the first place.

By not compromising or even letting him know what my systems were, we were unable to deal with the realities of living together again. I was unable to compromise for two reasons: I was in denial that I had to have things done my way, and I was afraid he would be disappointed in me. I wanted to believe that I was so happy just to have him home that I could be flexible with everything else, other than my routines. This obviously was not true. As independent as I had become, I was still worried about what he thought about how I handled our life when he was gone. I did not want to open my self up to his opinions and make myself vulnerable. I had spent almost an entire year protecting my vulnerability from everyone. It was a hard habit to break.

Called to Duty

I did not want to open up to my husband because I did not feel safe. How could I be sure he would not have to leave again? Even if he was never activated again, how could I be sure he would not have a tragic accident? Obviously I had a long way to go towards being intimate again, but first we had to deal with our daily routines. We had to figure out a way to coexist again.

It was a lot easier when he started working. A lot of returning soldiers were able to go back to their same old life. My husband wasn't able to because he was a student who came back a month too late. He had to wait another year to pick up where he left off with his education. In the mean time, he had to find a meaningful way to spend his time in order to feel productive. That took longer then expected, but we were not able to peacefully coexist without it. He had to work on his own issues like I had to work on mine. We also had the help of a professional, which I would highly recommend to anyone. We did not see the counselor for very long, but it was helpful to talk to an unbiased third party.

So we found a routine and started to communicate better. What ever happened to our magical reunion with our long vacation somewhere secluded? It was one of many expectations and fantasies I had to finally let go of if I were going to live happily with my husband again. That was the final emotional obstacle I confronted about the deployment. I had developed many expectations about how I would be, how he would be, and how we would be together. Most of them I pulled out of my imagination and they were far from reality. They were off base because they dealt mostly with my fantasies and not those of my partner. The vacation was a good example. I never considered that all my husband would want to do when he got home would be to stay home. I also never assumed that we would fight all the time about trivial things.

Once I accepted that my predictions and hopes would not come to fruition, I was able to begin living in the moment. This was the only way I was able to experience some true happiness. I finally realized that I can't predict the future and I cannot change what happened in the past. I was able to let go and be happy about being with the person

Called to Duty

I care about the most. I was finally able to feel his arms around me and shed all of the bitterness, loneliness, and despair.

Settling in Again

☙

So now that I am finally able to live in the moment and let go of my expectations, what next? I needed to accept that it was okay for me, my husband, and our lives to be different. We had spent a year growing and changing. We were bound to learn new things and evolve into different people. I had developed a newfound independence, while he decided to rethink some of his priorities.

Our relationship changed as well. I didn't need to be with him every minute of every day and he appreciated my company a little more. This allowed for us to meet some where in the middle and live quite happily. At first we both had the tendency to judge each other by our past behavior. It took a while for us to see the differences and realize how beneficial they were.

We benefited from this interesting and torturous experience. There were definitely some lessons learned from the deployment. Lesson number one: We need each other because we love each other and we don't love each other because we need each other. It became clearly obvious after functioning for so long in my daily life without my husband that I was pretty self-sufficient. I could survive just fine without him and he could survive without me. It also became clearly apparent that we needed each other because life was emotionally void without my husband. I needed to have him around because I enjoyed his company and I enjoyed being who I was when I was with him. I found I didn't need him around to survive, but I did need him around to be happy.

Lesson number two: People can handle more than they imagine. I was able to tolerate an unimaginably long separation from my husband. After going through the pain of him leaving for boot camp, I thought I would

Called to Duty

kill myself if he was ever deployed. But I didn't and I am still a relatively healthy and functioning human being. I found that I had strength in places I did not realize existed. I discovered a newfound fortitude in myself that helped me get through life's other trials with confidence.

Lesson number three: Your true friends accept you for who you are. I became a very strange and often hard person to deal with throughout this experience. My real friends accepted my behavior and understood where I was coming from. I was not afraid that I would loose them because of my many personalities during the deployment. Luckily, they realized the trial I was going through and they gave me more than they got from me in return. I will always keep these people as close friends because I know they are *true friends*.

Lesson number four: When it comes down to it, you have to help yourself. I realized that with all of the outside support I had I was still feeling that they did not understand me completely. That is because they did not. They could not. Deep down I knew what I needed and when I needed it, and it was up to me to get it. If I needed to be alone, I made sure I was left alone. If I needed support from somebody, I had to make sure I sought it out. I found out that people were not able to read my mind, and that if I was going to survive the deployment, I needed to help myself. This was one of the harder lessons to learn. I spent a lot of time being resentful at different people in my life because they were not "helping" me. It took a while for me to realize that I had to let them know how to help me.

Lesson number five: People don't always realize when they are being offensive. I realized that most of the things people said that hurt me were actually meant to be nice and supportive. Sometimes people don't know what to say or how to say it. I either had to accept their good intentions or speak up and let them know what they said hurt me. When I got tired of the pain I felt every time someone asked when my husband was coming home, I simply told them to stop asking and I would let them know when I knew. Eventually, as I got used to my new routines, I was able to not take such questions personally.

Lesson number six: Nobody is perfect. I learned that fact the hard way. I did all sorts of crazy things outside of my normal behavior, attempting to cope with my problems. I was extremely hard on myself, but looking back, I am able to realize that I was trying to figure out the best way to deal with my many issues. I eventually found a balance of social life, work, and painful loneliness that allowed me to cope until my husband returned home. I had to ease up on myself and realize that I am not perfect even though I might think I have to be.

Lesson number seven: It is okay to get professional help. I found that seeing counselors during especially rough patches helped me find the path again. It was so much easier to see what I needed by having and unbiased third-party tell me their observations. Therapy was definitely worth it.

Lesson number eight: My problems affect our problems, his problems affect our problems and our problems affect my problems etc… I realized that I could not separate my issues from what we were dealing with as a couple. My husband had to realize the same. Once we understood that we had to confront everything at once rather than tackle one thing at a time we were able to make progress. At first we would always drag each other back into the same communication problems because we did not fix what we had within ourselves. Once we recognized that it was the whole system that needed fixing, we affected all areas that were not functioning. By acknowledging this connection, we saw changes in all areas of our lives and not just the ones we were trying to "fix".

Lesson number nine: Communication, communication, communication! Throughout this entire process communication was the key problem and problem solver. While he was leaving, while he was gone, while he was coming home, and when he was living at home again, it was important that we both communicated openly and honestly. We found this to be a lot harder than it sounds. We had to stop protecting our partner from our emotions and let the other person know what was going. If we did not, then the problem grew and festered inside until it eventually burst out. Working it out before the explosion was easier to do even though it felt like the riskier option. Now we have gotten ourselves in the habit of diffusing explosions and it leads to a much smoother home life.

Lesson number ten: Honesty is the best policy. This follows very closely with communication. Being honest with your partner saves a lot of grief later. Being honest with yourself helps as well. By having all the cards out on the table you are able to adequately assess what is necessary and what needs to be done. It takes a lot more emotional energy to hide the truth than to deal with it.

And finally, lesson number eleven: We can make it through anything. This whole experience has taught us the most important thing of all: that we have what it takes to make it through anything life decides to throw at us, and that our relationship is worth fighting for. Like any tough situation in life, this has shown us both what we are made of and that we can handle it. While I wouldn't ever choose to willingly go through this experience, at least I know now that we truly love each other and that this isn't a fairytale.

What an interesting test fate has given many National Guard families. They have to learn an awful lot to pass and they don't always pass the first time. If you are lucky you might stumble upon a path to success. I know I wasn't prepared for this and I truly feel that I was lucky to be able to work it out. Not everyone is so lucky. My husband and I are not only taking all of these valuable lessons with us from this experience, we are also taking a new view of the way the world works. Life is not fair. You do what you can to be a good person and do the right thing, but that does not insure you against wrongdoing. In both my life and my job I see the inability to control our life's path. Sometimes you cannot stop what happens. Sometimes you have to accept it and cope the best you can. Believe me -- you can. While you cannot control your life, you are able to make decisions to proceed in positive or negative directions. Despite this gloomy vision of the way the world is, we still realize that we have it good and can continue to make positive choices. We need to appreciate what we have when we have it. Living in the moment is the only true way to enjoy life. You cannot change what has happened to you. You can't predict what will happen to you.

You can only deal with what you are getting from life at the present, and presently my husband is home and we are enjoying each other's company. I didn't think we would, but we made it through.

References

Kubler-Ross, E. (1969). **On death and dying.** New York, NY: Scribner.

Seligman, M. (1998). **Learned optimism: How to change your mind and your life.** New York, NY: Free Press

Printed in the United States
143724LV00001B/4/A